"This upbeat series really encourages the very young to 'go for it!' with bright vocabulary, illustration and concept . . . These lovely books are true boosters for preschool confidence, self-concept and beginning reading skills."

—*School Library Journal*

Bear is all set to eat a good lunch—but that's not so easy. The soup spills all over his bib, the jam spreads all over the table, and the spaghetti just won't be tamed! "Eating," Bear realizes, "is harder than I thought. What do I do now?"

Bear's messy—but very delicious—solution is sure to delight young children, many of whom may well be struggling for the first time with eating their own lunch "all by themselves."

SHIGEO WATANABE, editor and author of many outstanding books for young people, is nearly as well-known in this country as he is in his native Japan. In 1977, he was chosen to deliver the prestigious May Hill Arbuthnot Honor Lecture. Mr. Watanabe is also Japan's representative to the Executive Committee of the International Board on Books for Young People (IBBY), and has translated many of the world's great children's books into Japanese.

An acclaimed illustrator, YASUO OHTOMO, brings to this book the warmth, simplicity, and humor for which he is especially known and loved. Both he and Mr. Watanabe live near Tokyo.

I Can Do It All By Myself
books by
Shigeo Watanabe

How do I put it on?
AN AMERICAN LIBRARY ASSOCIATION
NOTABLE CHILDREN'S BOOK

What a good lunch!

Get set! Go!

I'm the king of the castle!

I can ride it!

Where's my daddy?

I can build a house!

I can take a walk!

Text copyright © 1978 by Shigeo Watanabe
Illustrations copyright © 1978 by Yasuo Ohtomo
American text copyright © 1980 by William Collins Publishers, Inc.
All rights reserved
Published in the United States by Philomel Books
a division of The Putnam & Grosset Book Group
200 Madison Avenue, New York, NY 10016
Printed in Hong Kong
Library of Congress CIP information at back of book

What a good lunch!

Story by Shigeo Watanabe Pictures by Yasuo Ohtomo

PHILOMEL BOOKS

I can eat lunch all by myself.

Soup first. Shall I drink it?

No! I should have used my spoon.

Bread and butter next.

I'll use my spoon and fork.

No! That must be wrong.

Strawberry jam. Do I pour it on?

No! It's coming out too fast!

Spaghetti. That looks easy.

Oh, no! I can't seem to catch any.

Eating is harder than I thought.

What do I do now?

I know. I'll put the soup on
the spaghetti.

And the bread and salad on
top of that.

Then I'll eat it all with my fingers.

What a good lunch!

I ate it all by myself!

Library of Congress Cataloging in Publication Data
Watanabe, Shigeo, 1928–   What a good lunch!
(An I can do it all by myself book; 2)
SUMMARY: Despite difficulties, a young bear eats
his lunch all by himself.
[1. Table etiquette—Fiction.   2. Etiquette—Fiction.
3. Bears—Fiction]   I. Ohtomo, Yasuo.   II. Title.
PZ7.W2615Wf [E] 79-19535
ISBN 0-399-21846-7 (GB)
ISBN 0-399-21845-9 (pbk)
First GB Edition (revised)
First Paperback Edition (revised)